Spend a Day
on the Farm

Hello! My name is Molly and this is my little brother, Sam. We live with our family on Swallowdale Farm. Let's go around the farm together and we can show you what goes on.

We have lots of animals for you to see—ducks, chickens, sheep, cows, horses, and many others as well.

Our farm dog, Flash, might come along. He knows a lot about the farm but he's a little bit shy!

Fold out for a map of the farm and a DVD!

chicken run

First, we'll take you to see the chickens. They live in the orchard near our farmhouse, where they have lots of space to run around freely.

When Sam and I feed grain to the chickens, the whole flock comes running. They peck at the corn and use their strong claws to scratch the ground looking for food.

All of our chickens have had their wings clipped to stop them from flying away.

Watch the chicks on DVD

🐓 Chicken facts

- A group of chickens is called a flock
- A male chicken is called a rooster
- A female chicken is called a hen
- A baby chicken is called a chick

5

Henhouse

Every morning as the Sun rises, our noisy rooster wakes up the whole farm with his crowing! He's easy to spot because he's the largest bird in the flock. Can you see his bright red comb and long, curly tail feathers?

Today, Sam's helping me put clean straw bedding in the henhouse. We do this about once a week.

comb

beak

tail feather

wattle

wing

claw

Watch the hens on
DVD

6

Egg collecting

During the day, the hens take turns visiting the henhouse and laying their eggs in the cozy nesting box.

My job is to collect the eggs each morning. I lift the lid of the nesting box as quietly as I can. Then I carefully hunt for the eggs hidden in the straw.

If we peek inside, we can see a hen sitting on its eggs. It will stay there until its chicks hatch.

Did you know?

A hen lays one egg a day. That means I have about 20 fresh eggs to collect each morning!

8

Duck pond

Let's go down to the pond, where the ducks spend their time swimming and diving. They dip their bills in the water looking for tasty weeds, snails, and insects to eat.

This cute little duckling I'm holding is just three days old! Its yellow feathers feel soft and fluffy. One day soon, it will follow its mother down to the pond for its first swim.

Watch the ducks on DVD

10

Lambing shed

Come and look inside the shed where the spring lambs are born. It's warm, dry, and very cozy. A mother sheep usually gives birth to twins or sometimes triplets!

At first, the lambs drink their mother's milk, which is full of the vitamins they need to grow strong. Later, they will also feed on hay and grass.

Our flock of sheep is very noisy. Each tiny lamb learns to listen for its mother's call and bleats back.

Watch the lambs on DVD

Sheep facts

- A group of sheep is called a flock
- A male sheep is called a ram
- A female sheep is called a ewe
- A baby sheep is called a lamb

12

13

14

sheep field

Let's visit the sheep out in the field. Here the flock can graze on fresh, green grass. Our spring lambs are really playful as they run, skip, and jump around. It's fun to race them across the field.

The sheep grow a thick, woolly coat, called a fleece. This keeps them warm when the weather turns cold.

Watch the sheep on DVD

woolly fleece

ear

muzzle

leg

hoof

15

Haymaking

At the beginning of summer, when the weather is sunny and dry, it's haymaking time. Flash and I go up to the fields and watch the tractor mow the grass.

Once the grass has dried out, it is called hay and it is tied into bales and left in the fields, ready to be picked up. Sam and I love playing on the hay bales and watching Flash jump over them.

Sometimes, at the end of the day, we sit on the tractor and pretend to drive it.

Did you know?

Grass is turned into hay to feed sheep and cattle in the winter months.

17

cow meadow

Our small herd of cows lives in the meadow not far from the farmyard. In the summer, they spend all day in the field just grazing. In the winter, when the weather is cold, they are brought into the cow shed.

Cows need good grass to make lots of rich milk to feed their calves.

Did you know?

The fresh milk we drink comes from cows. On dairy farms, the cows are milked by machine twice a day. The milk is taken to a dairy, where it is put into cartons or turned into butter, cream, yogurt, cheese, and yummy ice cream.

Goat pen

We keep Gertie, our big nanny goat, and her kids indoors during bad weather. Sam and I love playing in the straw with the little kids.

Goats are great climbers and they are always trying to escape from their pen. We had to build a really strong fence to keep them in.

Gertie is milked by hand twice a day. We collect her creamy milk and use it to make cheese.

Watch the goats on DVD

21

woodland pigs

Follow me up to the woods to see where our pigs live. They love snoozing and spend most of the day lying around in the shade of the trees.

The rest of the time, they wander around the woods, digging their snouts in the soil looking for grubs, worms, roots, and plants to eat.

Look at our pig scratching its itchy back on the fence.

Watch the pigs on DVD

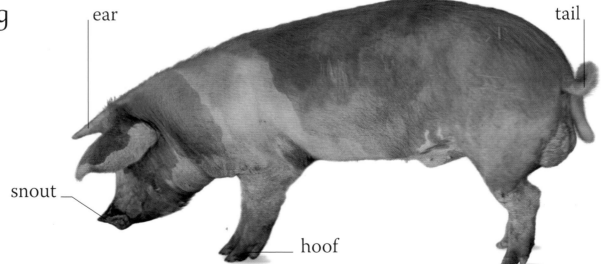

ear

tail

snout

hoof

23

Pig arcs

Look inside the arcs, where the pigs shelter from the hot Sun and keep warm in the cold. This is where our huge sow lives with her litter of ten hungry piglets. The piglets still suckle milk from their mother, but they enjoy rooting in the soil, too.

This tiny piglet is the runt of the litter. This means that it is the smallest piglet. It is my job to make sure it gets enough food.

 ## Pig facts

- A group of pigs is called a herd
- A male pig is called a boar
- A female pig is called a sow
- A baby pig is called a piglet

Watch the pigs on DVD

25

Horse paddock

I love visiting the horses in the paddock. They graze on sweet meadow grass. Sometimes I feed them their favorite treat—carrots and apples.

This is my very own pony, named Chestnut—I'm still learning how to ride her.

It feels very high up when I'm sitting in the saddle, but I'm not scared, because Chestnut knows to stop walking when I pull on the reins.

I also wear a riding hat to protect my head in case of a fall.

Watch the horses on DVD

Horse stables

After I've been for a ride, I take Chestnut back to the stables. Here, there is lots of work for me to do. First, I take off her saddle and then the bridle.

Chestnut nibbles away on hay, while I groom her body and tail thoroughly with a special brush called a body brush. Afterward, her coat looks all clean and shiny.

 Horse facts

- A male horse is called a stallion
- A female horse is called a mare
- A baby horse is called a foal
- A small horse is called a pony

Watch the horses on DVD

29

Goodbye from Swallowdale Farm

Well, now it's time for us to say goodbye. We hope you've enjoyed your trip around Swallowdale Farm. Don't forget to look at our special DVD to see all the animals in action.

Please come back and visit us again soon. Sam, Flash, and I will be waiting for you!

MOLLY
XX